DO NOT STAND SO CLOSE TO ME

Poems by Shomshuklla

Rupa & Co

Published 2011 by
Rupa Publications India Pvt. Ltd.
7/16, Ansari Road, Daryaganj,
New Delhi 110 002

Sales Centres:

Allahabad Bengaluru Chennai
Hyderabad Jaipur Kathmandu
Kolkata Mumbai

Designed by Sanjay Shaw
(shaws007@gmail.com)

Illustrated by Sanjay Shaw

Organised by
Genesis Advertising Pvt. Ltd.

Printed in India by
Nutech Photolithographers
B-240, Okhla Industrial Area, Phase-I,
New Delhi 110 020

I dedicate this book to my son, Rik, who is turning into a nice and a warm young man, by coincidence, he is my son, but in reality, my true friend, to share my love, grief and pain. What else can I ask for?

Happy

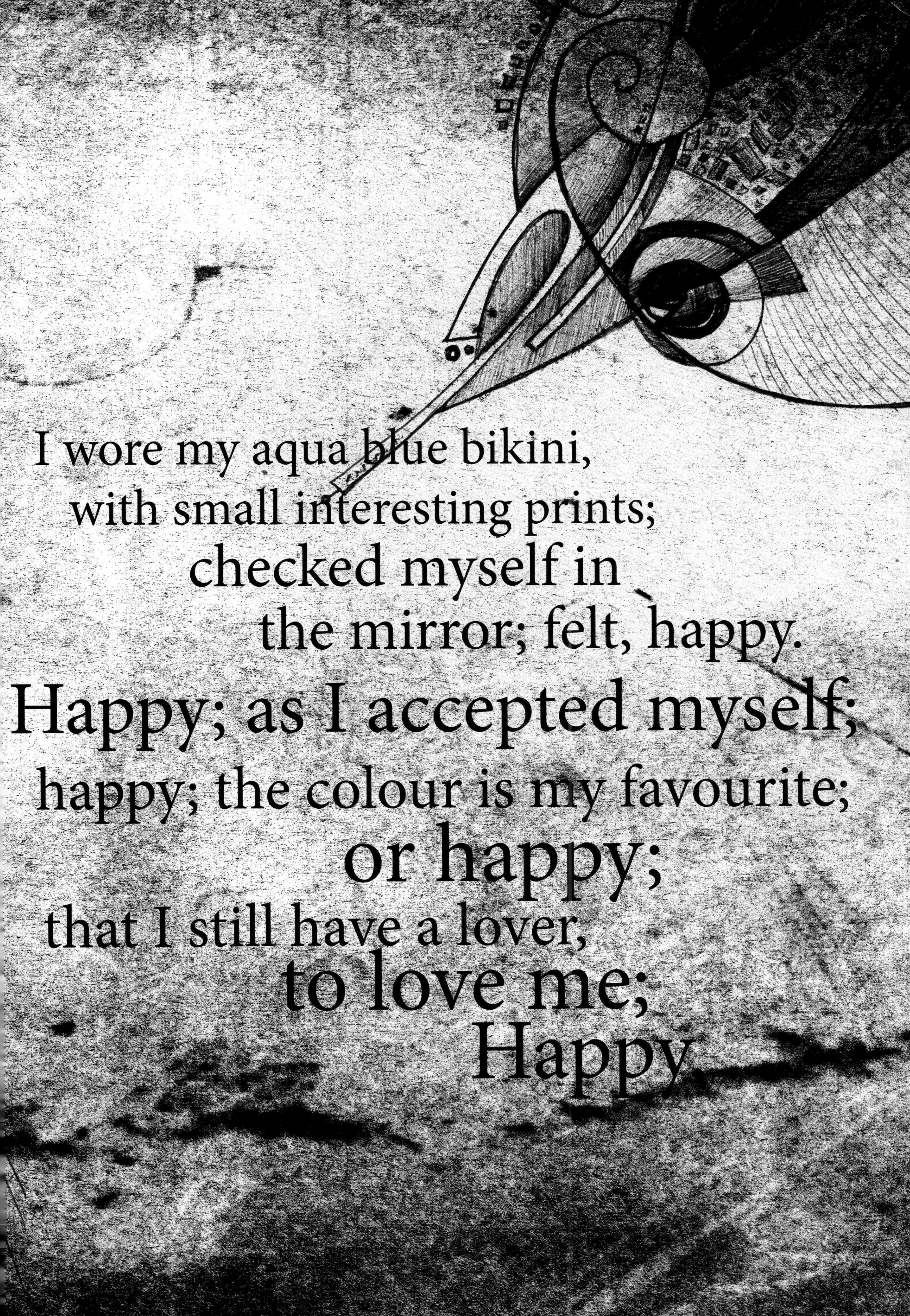

I wore my aqua blue bikini,
with small interesting prints;
checked myself in
the mirror; felt, happy.
Happy; as I accepted myself;
happy; the colour is my favourite;
or happy;
that I still have a lover,
to love me;
Happy

Promise

Don't ask for me –
Don't plead with me –
Don't fall in love
with me –
I heard you –
wait over that corner –
wait with love –

Bill

When you held my hand in that
moment, I was bewildered.
Looked at you to understand;
to know you well.
Saw your eyes; flushed with the
unknown knowledge.
Maybe you knew. Maybe not.
Didn't figure out who you are,
Do you think I can play
the role of the magician!
to solve!

Do I fit your bill!

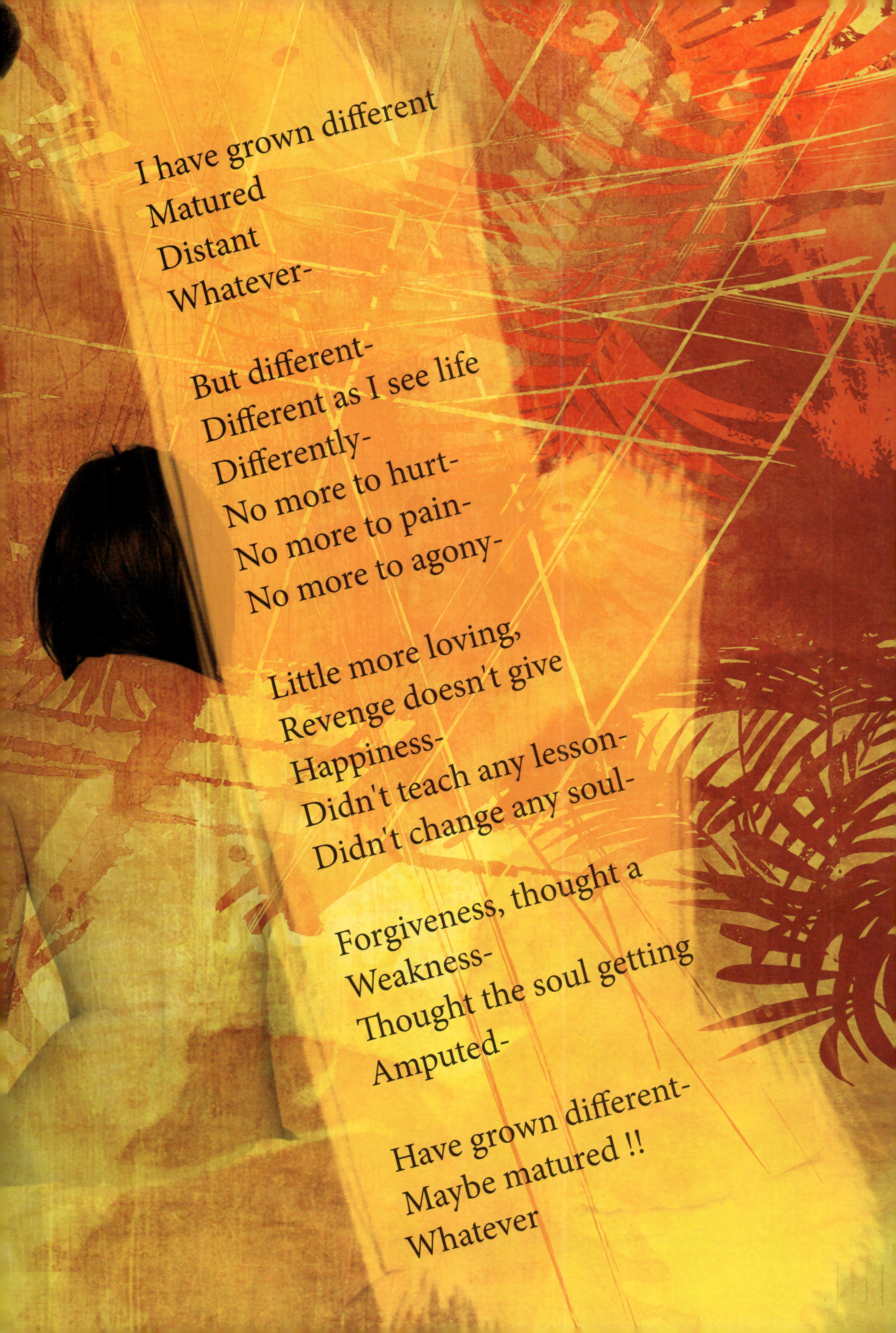

I have grown different
Matured
Distant
Whatever-

But different-
Different as I see life
Differently-
No more to hurt-
No more to pain-
No more to agony-

Little more loving,
Revenge doesn't give
Happiness-
Didn't teach any lesson-
Didn't change any soul-

Forgiveness, thought a
Weakness-
Thought the soul getting
Amputed-

Have grown different-
Maybe matured !!
Whatever

Smile

Oh! This is just a
jigsaw
puzzle –
Hey! Take the
pieces
put in order –
I turned my
face
looked on the other side
smiled –
a smile of achievement, success –
Yes! Jigsaw
Puzzle –
Pieces of a human of a character –
Broken, shattered,
ruined –
I smiled –
to glory – to victory
I smiled.

Measure

I was boiling water to have coffee,
was pondering over the

measurement of the coffee powder;
as I changed the size of the mug.
Now a vibrant large one from Nice.

While I was hesitating between the
coffee powder and the boiling water
in the electric kettle;
my cocker spaniel waited with dripping saliva,
eagerly,

her evening chocolate biscuit-
My favourite with the coffee,
her with my company!

How we all measure,
form a structure.

Old

I sit in this old house –
watch its oldness –
doors,
make squeaking sound –
when opened –
Old arm chairs –
polished old –
The old window panes –
old tilled roof
old arched balcony –
Beautifully old –
all old –
Wondered!!
should I be
beautifully old

Sit

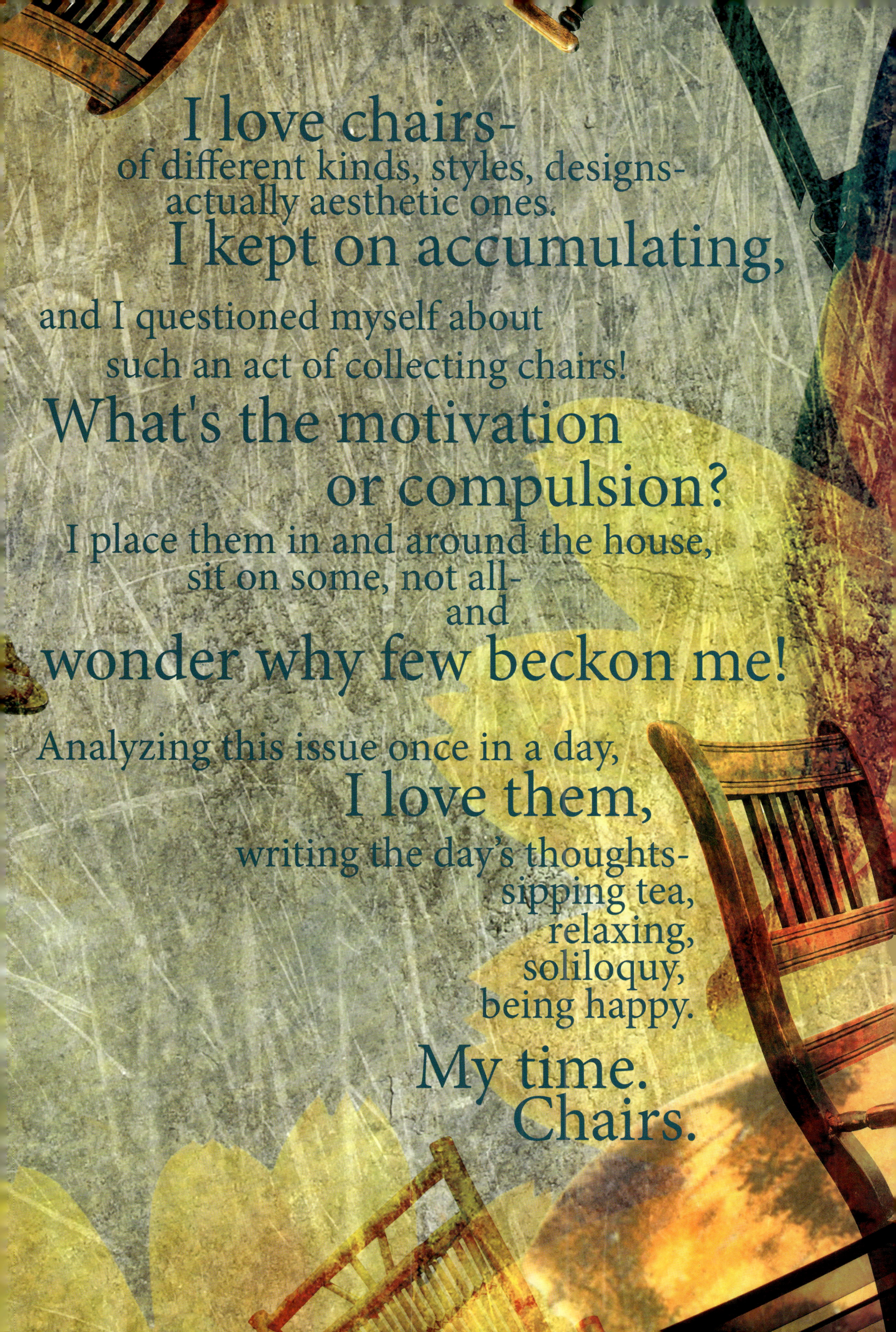
I love chairs-
of different kinds, styles, designs-
actually aesthetic ones.
I kept on accumulating,
and I questioned myself about
such an act of collecting chairs!
What's the motivation
or compulsion?
I place them in and around the house,
sit on some, not all-
and
wonder why few beckon me!
Analyzing this issue once in a day,
I love them,
writing the day's thoughts-
sipping tea,
relaxing,
soliloquy,
being happy.
My time.
Chairs.

Before

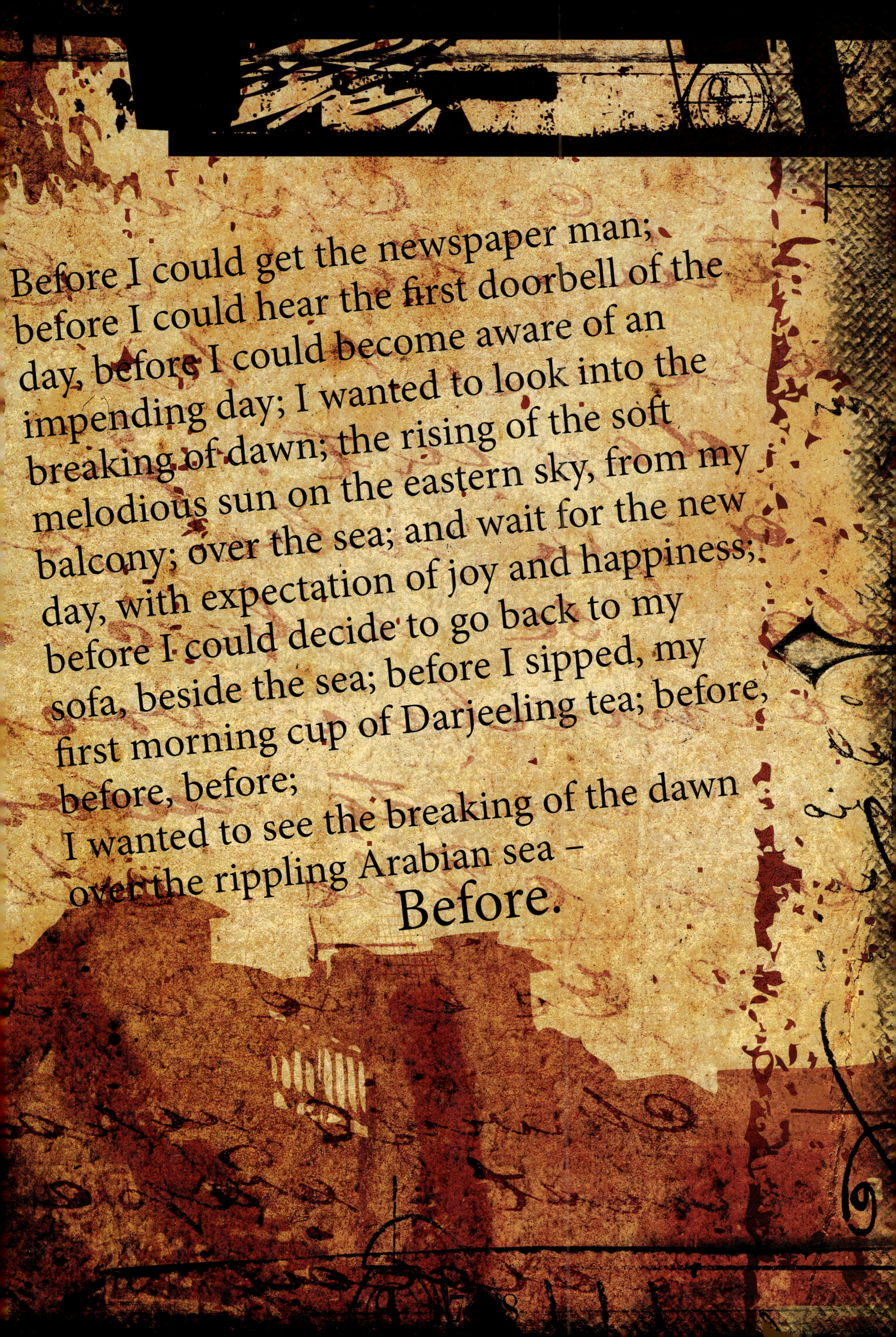

Before I could get the newspaper man;
before I could hear the first doorbell of the
day, before I could become aware of an
impending day; I wanted to look into the
breaking of dawn; the rising of the soft
melodious sun on the eastern sky, from my
balcony; over the sea; and wait for the new
day, with expectation of joy and happiness;
before I could decide to go back to my
sofa, beside the sea; before I sipped, my
first morning cup of Darjeeling tea; before,
before, before;
I wanted to see the breaking of the dawn
over the rippling Arabian sea –
Before.

I know I want to run-
but don't know where to!
Which direction?
Don't know the path!
Stand alone on a black round spot
clueless!
All around is neither grass,
or desert, nor water-
just black, black
unknown space-
Can't even figure
out the horizon-

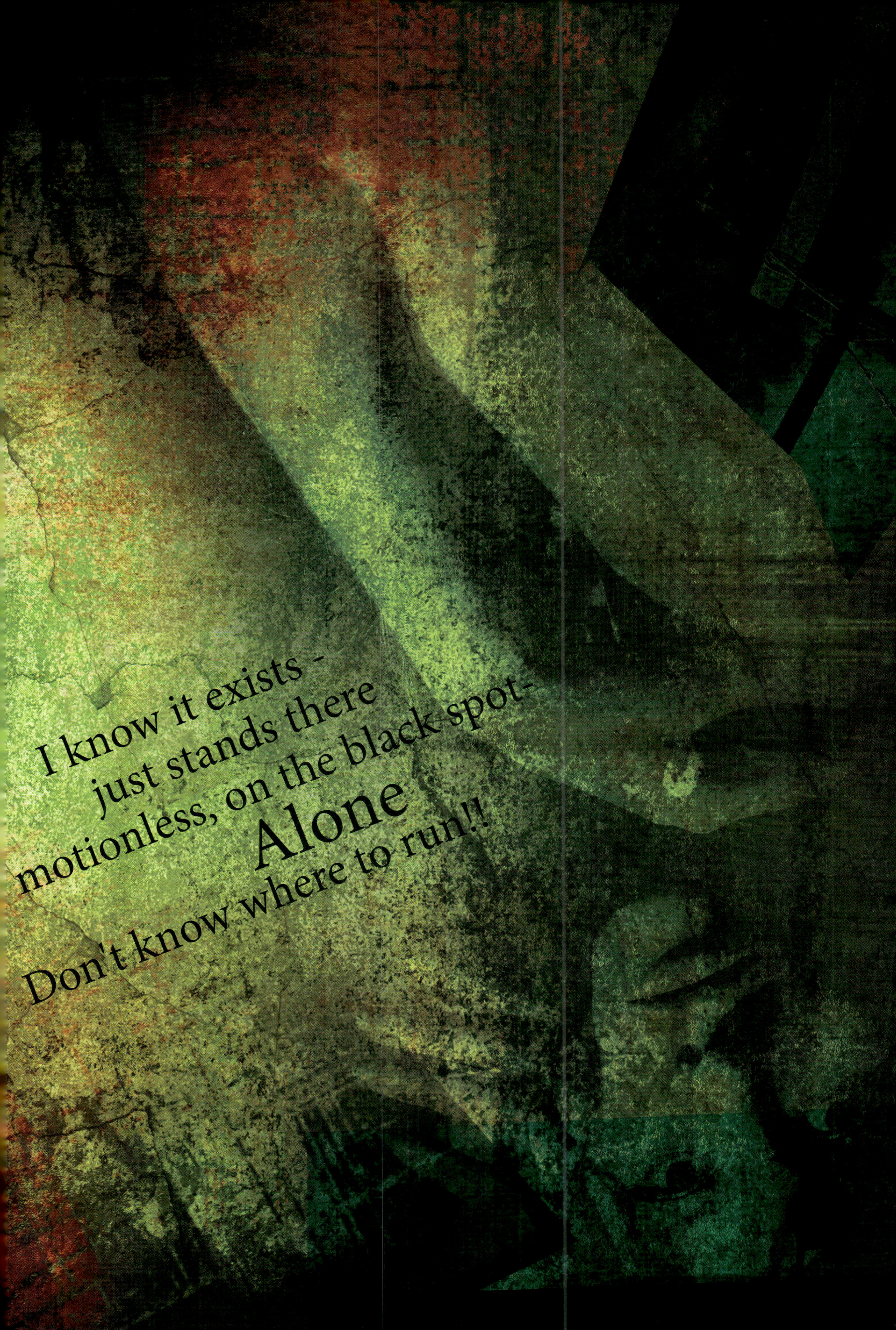
I know it exists -
just stands there
motionless, on the black spot-
Alone
Don't know where to run!!

Love

Forgot the words of love –
forgot its rhythm,
Its song –
Its beauty –
Looking, watching
to relearn,
Some tell me the truth,
some look lost,
some searching like me,
some don't know –
lucky though –
I, not so,
To relearn –
To find –
Love -

Fine

Hey! Yellow and red chrysanthemums –
don't look at me like that –
don't watch me.
You also don't look happy –
Your stems have
Become weak-
You are stooping –
Stop that;
Stop!
Don't look at me like that!
Don't!
I'm fine!
I'm.

Air

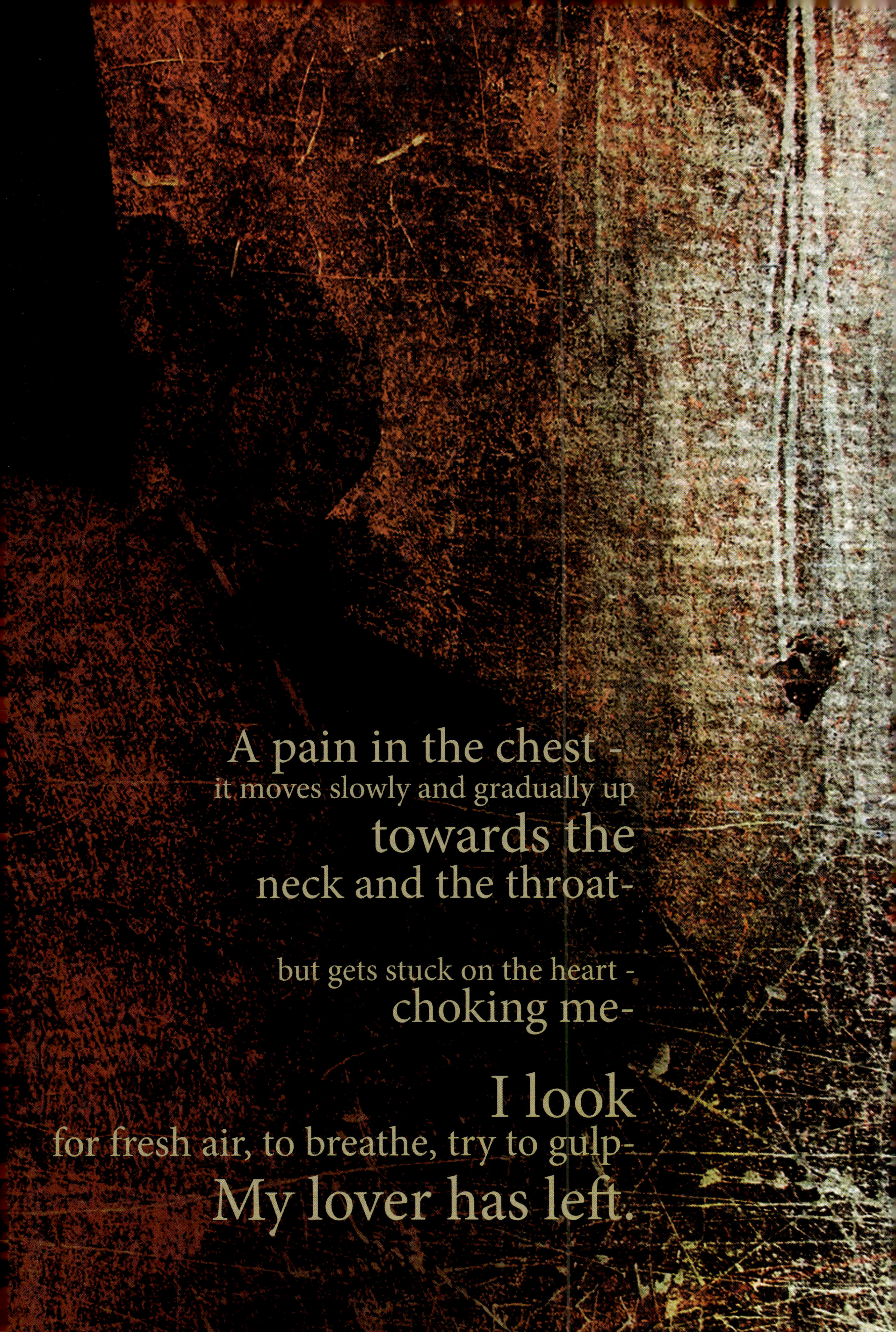
A pain in the chest -
it moves slowly and gradually up
towards the
neck and the throat-
but gets stuck on the heart -
choking me-
I look
for fresh air, to breathe, try to gulp-
My lover has left.

Images

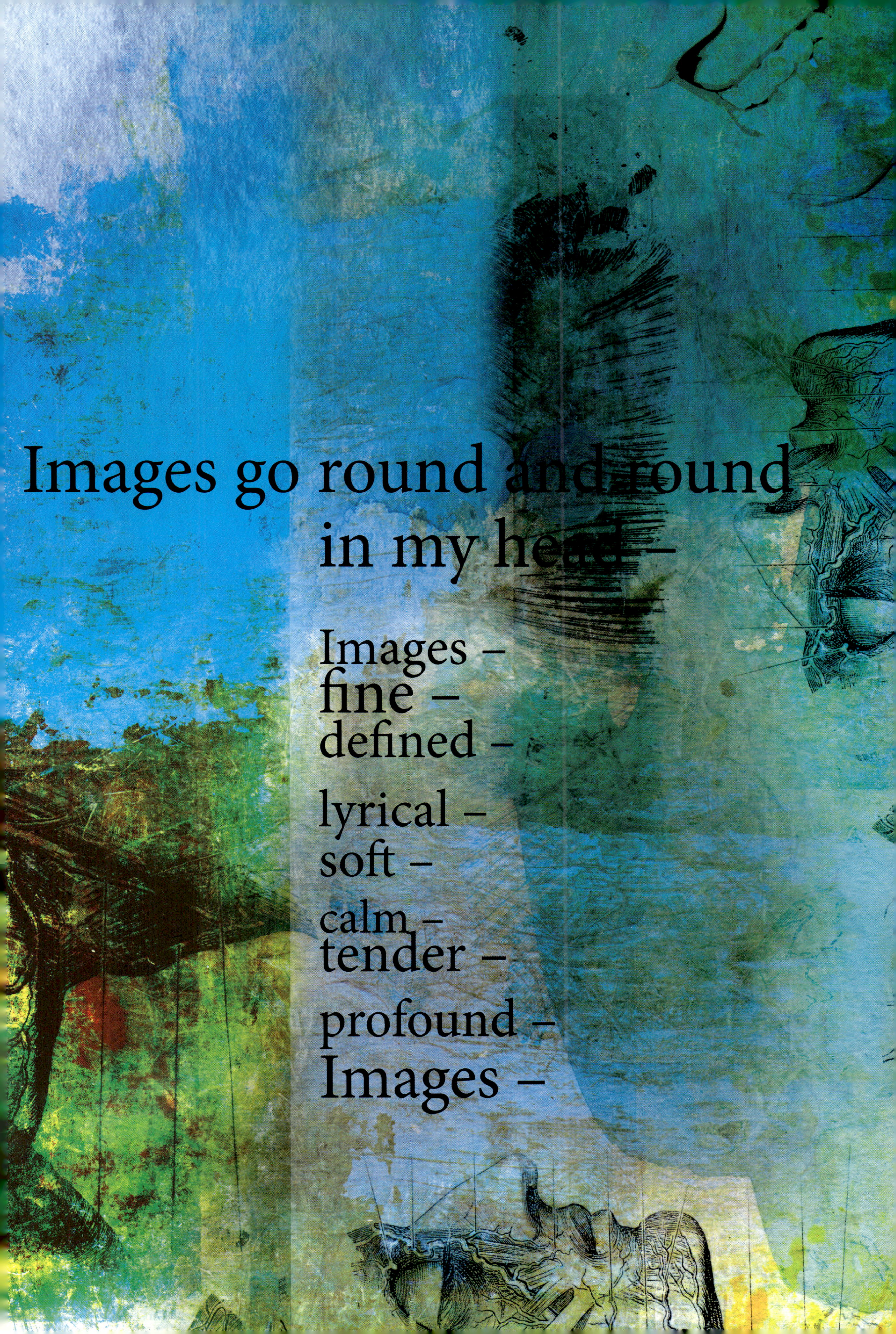

Images go round and round
in my head –

Images –
fine –
defined –

lyrical –
soft –
calm –
tender –
profound –
Images –

A smile lingers on my lips,
breaking into small little ones,
building again into another, new ones;
lots of it; like ripples on water;
a sunshine day; but the first rain;
in a bright sunny

day; like the first kiss;

my smile lingers;

lingers; seeing the rain; feeling of the first kiss –

Lingers,

Not pleasant

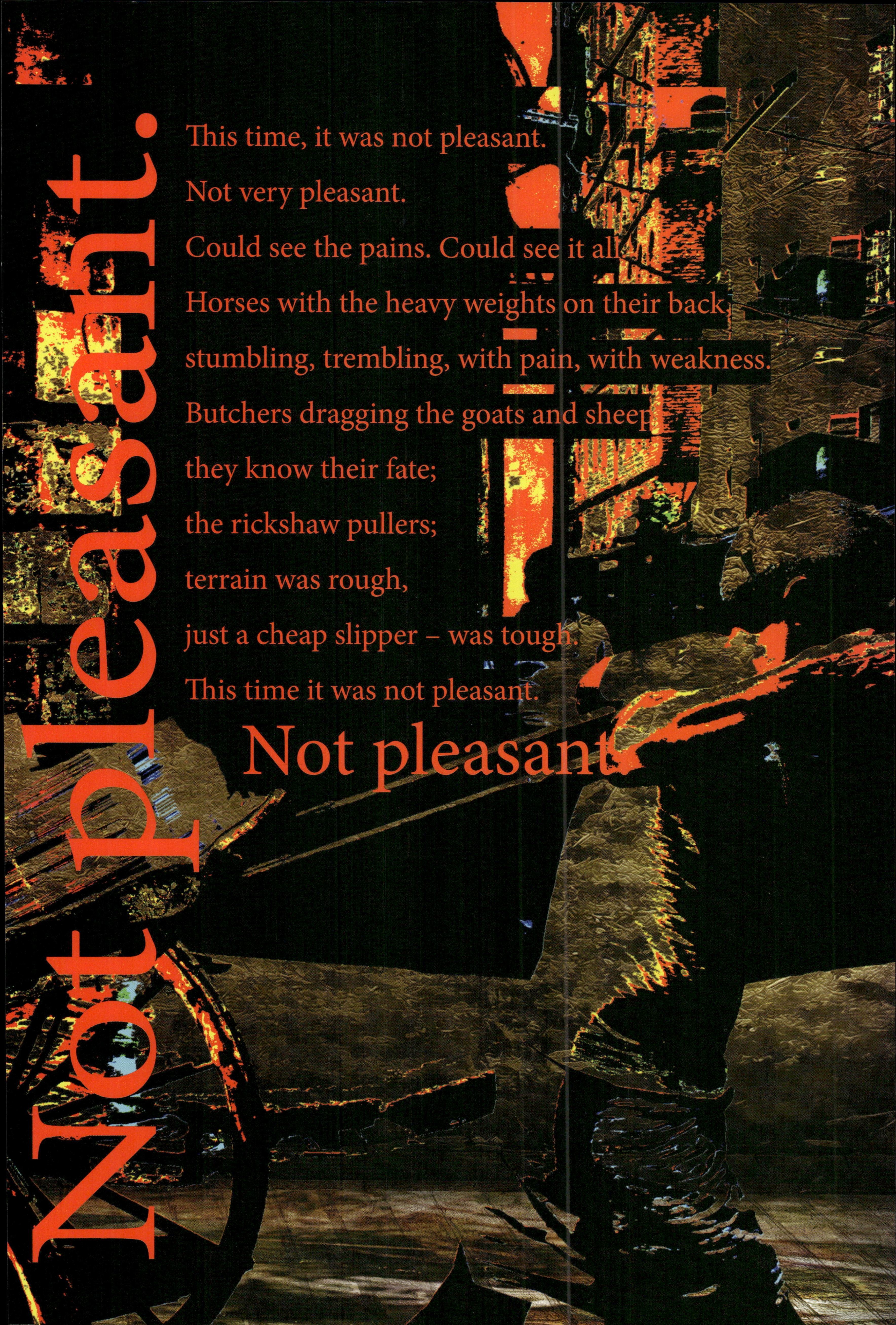
Not pleasant.
This time, it was not pleasant.
Not very pleasant.
Could see the pains. Could see it all.
Horses with the heavy weights on their back,
stumbling, trembling, with pain, with weakness.
Butchers dragging the goats and sheep,
they know their fate;
the rickshaw pullers;
terrain was rough,
just a cheap slipper – was tough.
This time it was not pleasant.
Not pleasant.

Stops me

I wish to hug you, but
something stops me.
Stops me, the moment I
think of it. Stops me. So
I turn to the other side
and try to get into a
dream. I'm good at it.
Very good weaving
dreams. I love it.
Weaving. But I try to
touch you in between my
dreams. But something

stops me.

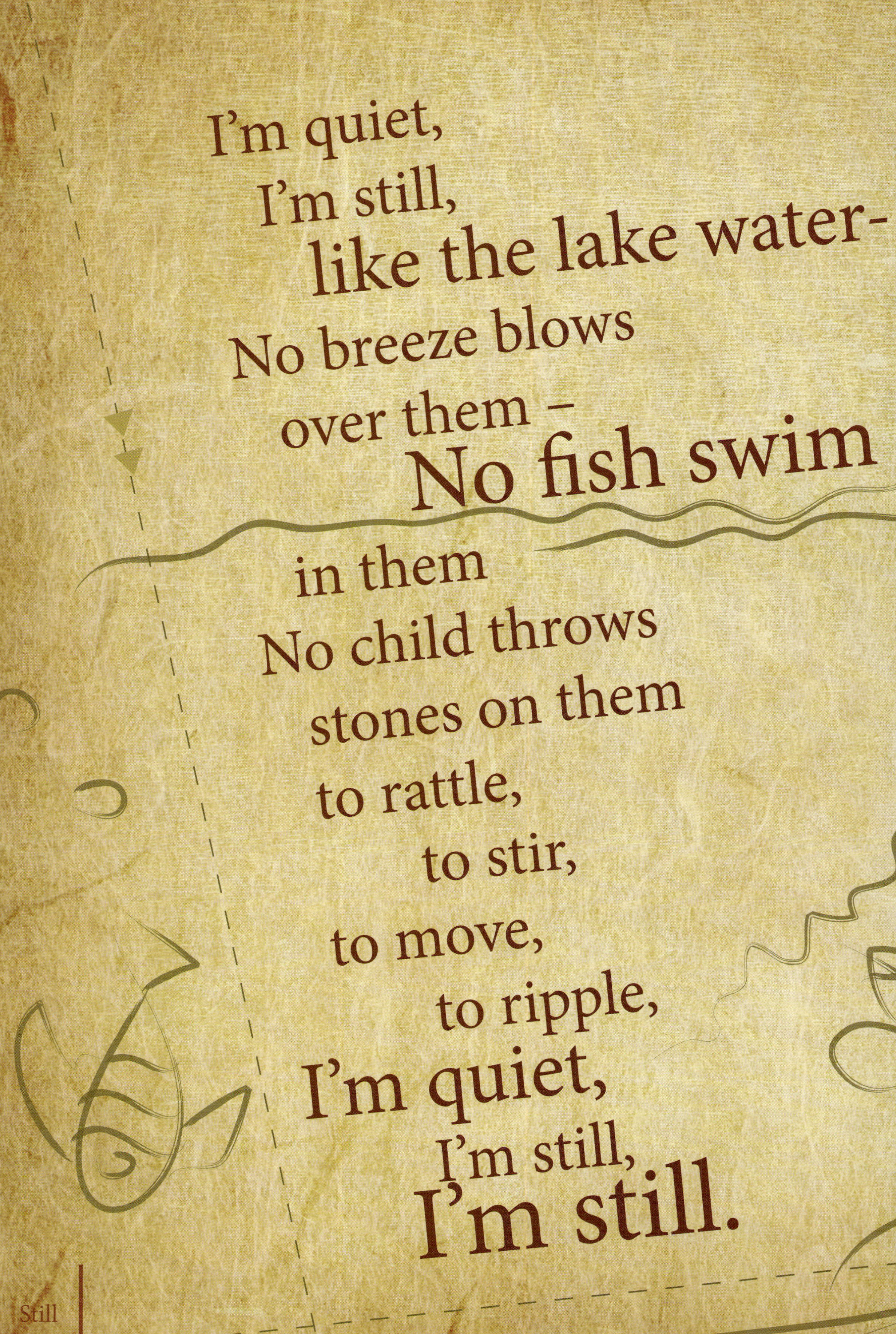

I'm quiet,
I'm still,
like the lake water-
No breeze blows
over them –
No fish swim
in them
No child throws
stones on them
to rattle,
to stir,
to move,
to ripple,
I'm quiet,
I'm still,
I'm still.

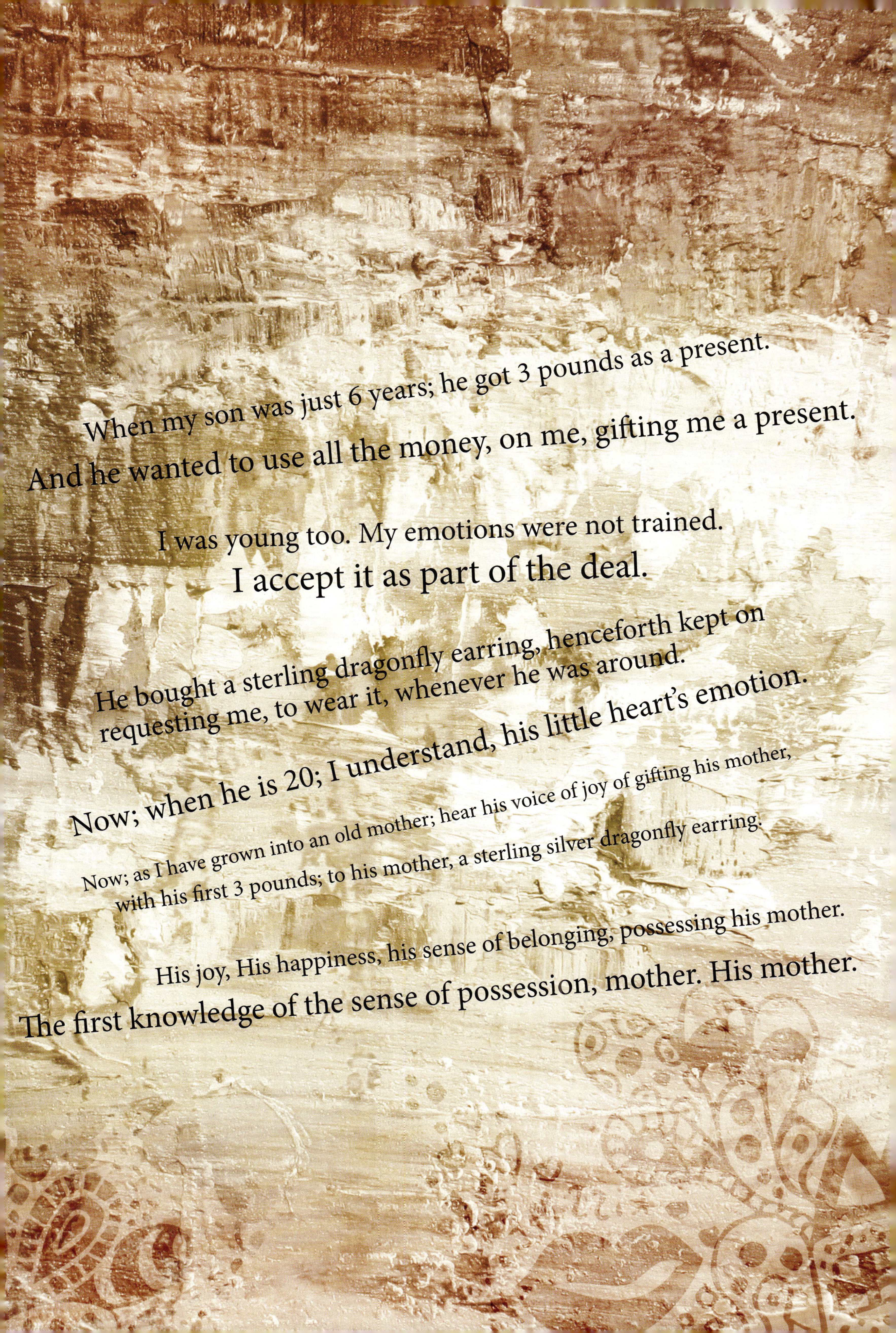

When my son was just 6 years; he got 3 pounds as a present.
And he wanted to use all the money, on me, gifting me a present.

I was young too. My emotions were not trained.
I accept it as part of the deal.

He bought a sterling dragonfly earring, henceforth kept on
requesting me, to wear it, whenever he was around.

Now; when he is 20; I understand, his little heart's emotion.

Now; as I have grown into an old mother; hear his voice of joy of gifting his mother,
with his first 3 pounds; to his mother, a sterling silver dragonfly earring.

His joy, His happiness, his sense of belonging, possessing his mother.
The first knowledge of the sense of possession, mother. His mother.

Watch

in a strange place; he held my hand; touched my lips;
I was away; watching him; trying to understand him;
he kissed me; I trying to understand him; he kissed me again; told me; he is not my lover; I watched him;
I watched him again;

I was away, I was away.

I watched him again.

Morning is cold,
Wrapped up in blanket.
Search for tiger.
Air is chilly,
Ranthambore.
Hard -
Yellow and black -
Wonderfully
camouflaged -
Eyes straining
he with his kill -
A black samba,
A magpie-Sitting on
a twig - above
Crying – crying…. Without rest -
crying -
Morning is cold,

Went walking over that uncharted path,
to my surprise, saw horses ,
many , grazing -
some looking towards the sky thoughtful;
some chewing
in their own pace, facing the grassland;
some trotting, alone-
auburn, black, white, red !

I love horses- their majesty,
mane, eyes, structure and grace!
Stopped to appreciate them
Suddenly felt a warm breath, enticing, turned to see-
a beautiful blue horse looking
towards me, welcoming a ride!

Rode him -
he wanted to ask me where to!
I smiled , sparkling , towards horizon -
We rode - down the uncharted path -
to our destination !!

That sole pigeon
came and sat
on the parapet.
Head was moving
In a rhythm,
Eyes red
with a black dot –
quill
grey, black
blue –
pink defined
claws –
Sole pigeon sat
on the parapet –
for sometime –
for sometime.

November

All this time I looked at life,
from my point of view-

But if I look at life from another
point of view, then life is good -

Just realized it made
me happy, content-

A bullock cart stationed, in Chowpatty-
the bullock undernourished, thin, chewing
the sugarcane - after the long pull,
thick wooden plank rubbing on the
raw shoulder - man thin like the bullock

But with a different
perspective -

Bullock could have been deserted and straying,
the man having no
business to sustain him,
begging on the roadside!

It was a bright sunny November morning-
I woke up with a happy dream -
Got a new perspective, to smile -

Sunny November morning.

Mirror reflects images.
Yes! It does.
What does this mirror talk!
What! What image
does it reflect!
Does it reflect the truth of a
human! Or the mere façade!

How does
it react to it!
Does it feel sad,
happy, free of
burden –

the burden of knowing
and seeing the truth,
the ugly truth!

The mirror
reflects images.

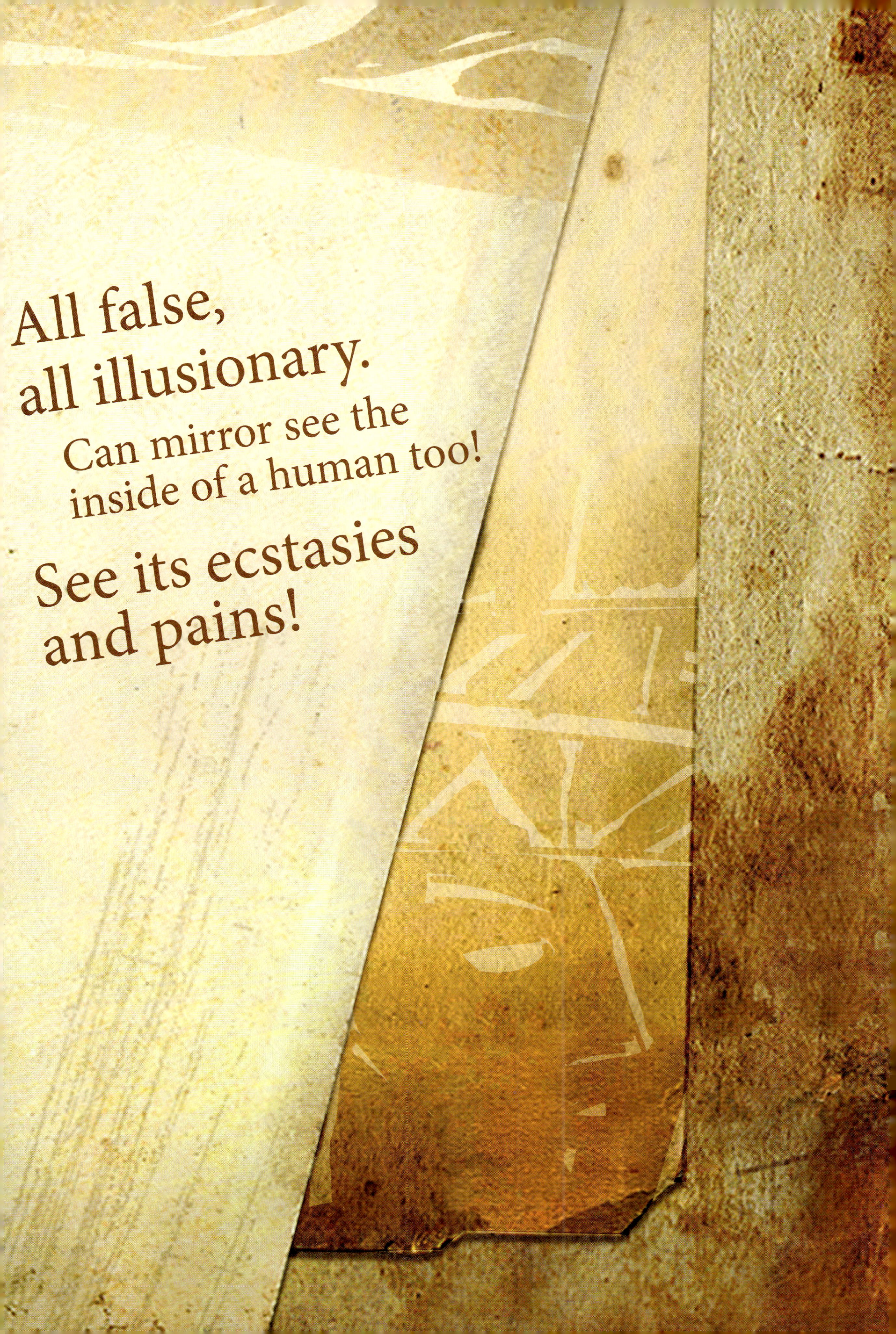
All false,
all illusionary.
Can mirror see the
inside of a human too!
See its ecstasies
and pains!

Should I sing for you?
Write poems!
allow you

to laugh with me!
Or just
look at you –

Smile
leave you

there –
to say
goodbye!

A Moment

Opened his suitcase and handed me-
a wrapped box a silver chain with a pendant-

The other day,
when I opened the drawer,

the box jumped out, seal unopened -
I smiled, putting it back in its place -
safe -

the silver chain -
a moment.

Demand

I want to sit down roll a joint-
want to smoke alone-
I don't want
any company-
human presence doesn't give me happiness-
creates a nuisance
around me-
I hate too many people-
hate people-
they don't know that-
I laugh
hysterically-
to look happy
I am not-
I act-
dramabazi-
to give eyewash
I hate people-
hypocrisy-
just want to be myself
Want to roll a joint-
smoke-
alone-
lie in the balcony-
look at the
sky-
day and night-
listen to the waves
I hate cacophony-
sound of cars-
moving up the hill
I want my father back-to love, understand-
want to tell all my pains, my hurt
I want to smoke a joint-
lie in the balcony
My space-
my life
A small demand.

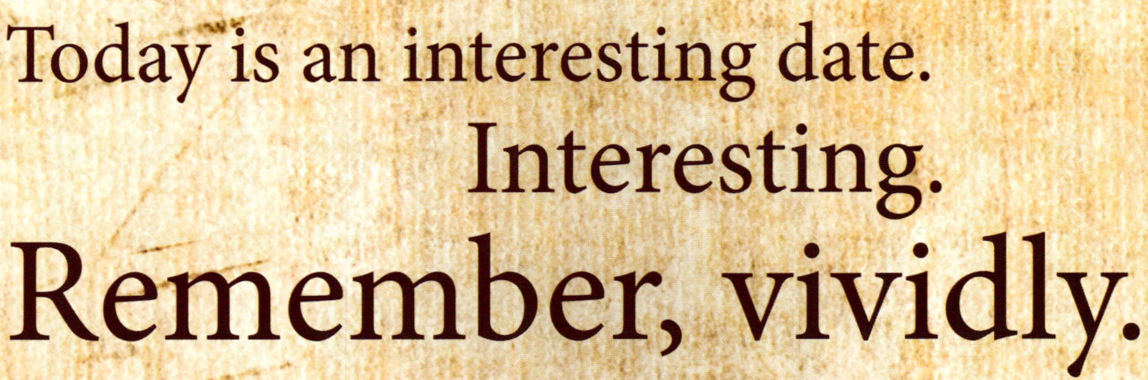
Today is an interesting date.
Interesting.
Remember, vividly.

Was with you,
Lots of fun.
Suddenly we looked at ourselves,
searched, different
paths; new life, like the growing of new grass;
we choose
to walk on that new road,
you on the right and I on the left.

We walked, we thought that
the road would end and
we could meet, but we
lost our ways; lost;

But the road will meet. We will embrace.
We will meet.

Freedom

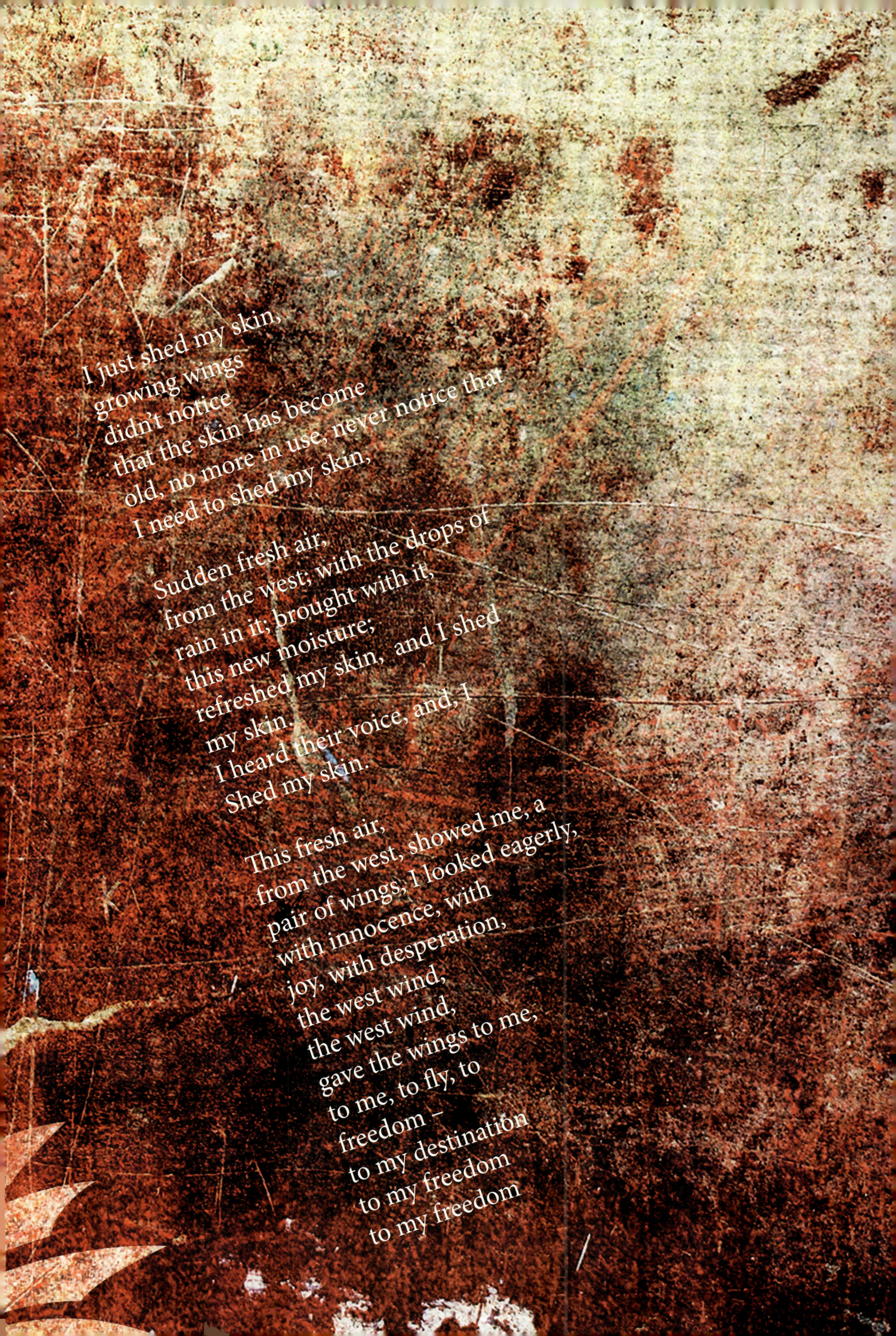

I just shed my skin,
growing wings
didn't notice
that the skin has become
old, no more in use, never notice that
I need to shed my skin,

Sudden fresh air,
from the west; with the drops of
rain in it; brought with it,
this new moisture;
refreshed my skin, and I shed
my skin.
I heard their voice, and, I
Shed my skin.

This fresh air,
from the west, showed me, a
pair of wings, I looked eagerly,
with innocence, with
joy, with desperation,
the west wind,
the west wind,
gave the wings to me,
to me, to fly, to
freedom –
to my destination
to my freedom
to my freedom

There is this constant sound, taking
birth in my house; television;
computer games; music system; dogs
bark; doorbell; ringing of the phone;
servants chatter; running of the air
conditioner;
Where will I get some –
Peace.
Quiet
Silence.
Sound. But no sound.

You wanted to walk,
you started walking;
thought the road is smooth;
flowing rivers;
flowers with beautiful fragrance;
when thirsty,
would drink the crystal clear water;
smell the flowers;
feel their tenderness;
rest on the green smooth grass,
then,
again,
walk on the soft, inviting road.
You thought the road is made
according to your wish –
You thought the road is made
according to your wish –

It is interesting to know you.
It's interesting your life, my life.
Magnetism,
like the solar system.
With energy, rotating in that maddening speed.
No spirituality, but an intoxication.
All engulfing.
Do we need to sit beside the seaside?
Go for a swim to soothe our agitated,
uncontrollable nerves!

What is the destiny!
What kind of a journey!
Do you have a plan?

Do we take a walk in the rain, holding hands,
feeling ourselves wet and
beautiful, ecstatic!
Or should we just start with a kiss,
to begin with and wait for the rest!!

Artificial...

I was laying the tarot cards. Not doing any mind reading or speculations. No. Not really. But as I sat on my sofa, looking out into the evening; evening fading into night; no I didn't notice, the twilight; I only noticed the evening, calmly, quietly, softly, fading into night; I looked out; intensely at the night; took my pen and started writing. Not writing a piece of ornamental sentence or thought; but just moments. Moments. Moments full of meaning. Full of life.

The night has fallen. Blue. Dark blue. While the white broad leaves lily, on the centre table; shiver a little in the air conditioned closed room; in the artificial breeze.

Artificial...

He

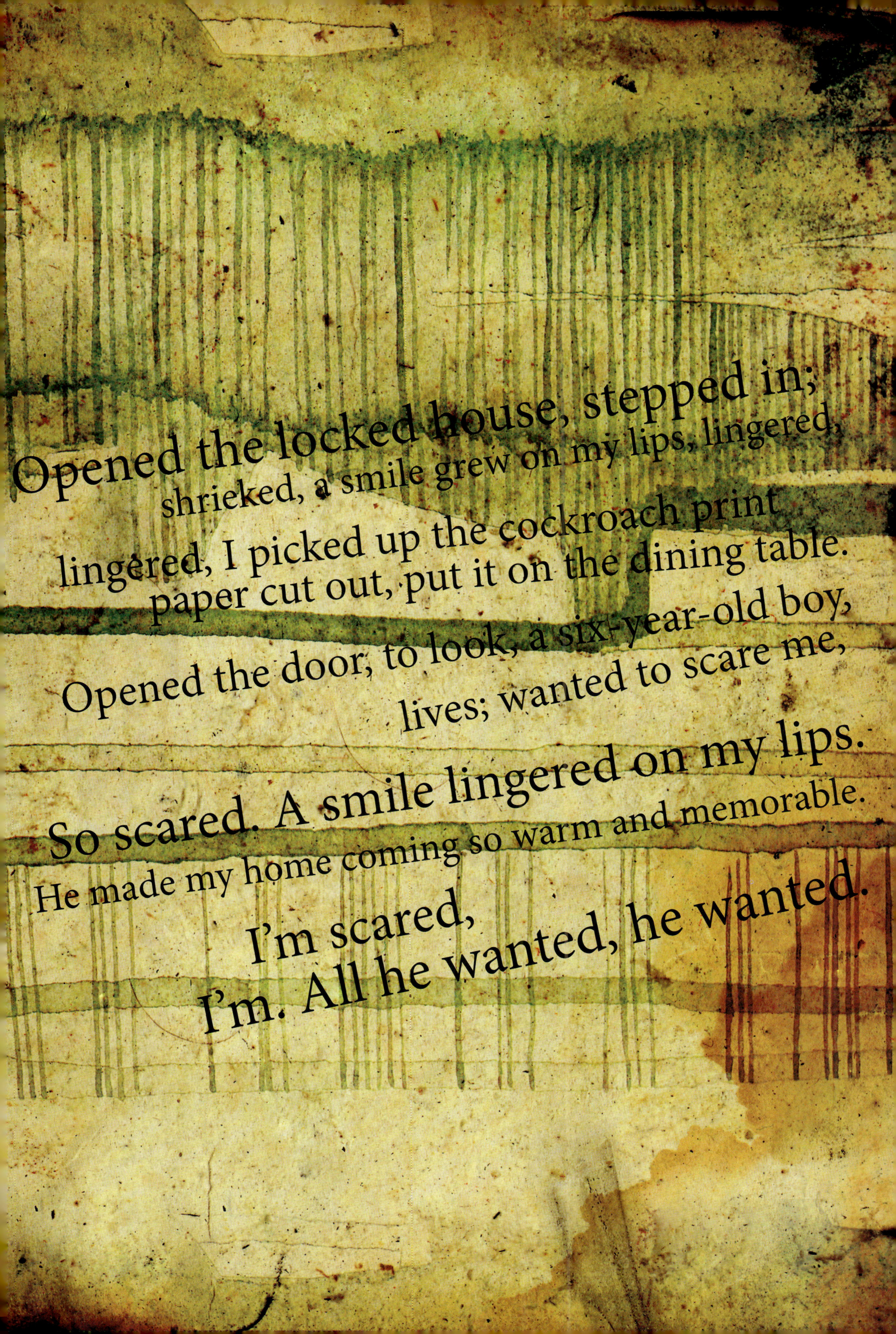
Opened the locked house, stepped in;
shrieked, a smile grew on my lips, lingered,
lingered, I picked up the cockroach print
paper cut out, put it on the dining table.
Opened the door, to look, a six-year-old boy,
lives; wanted to scare me,
So scared. A smile lingered on my lips.
He made my home coming so warm and memorable.
I'm scared,
I'm. All he wanted, he wanted.

Slowly

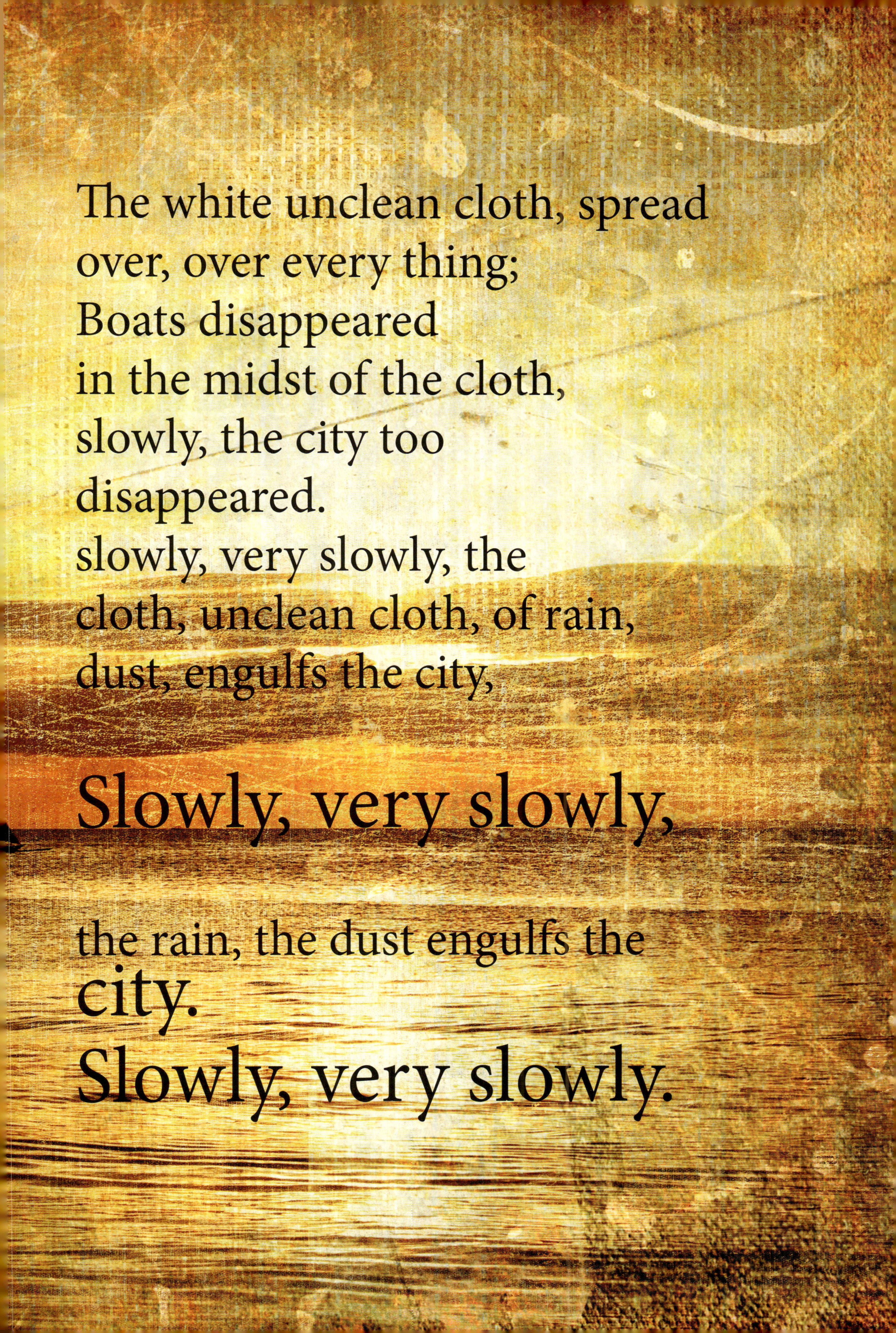

The white unclean cloth, spread
over, over every thing;
Boats disappeared
in the midst of the cloth,
slowly, the city too
disappeared.
slowly, very slowly, the
cloth, unclean cloth, of rain,
dust, engulfs the city,

Slowly, very slowly,

the rain, the dust engulfs the
city.
Slowly, very slowly.

Morning

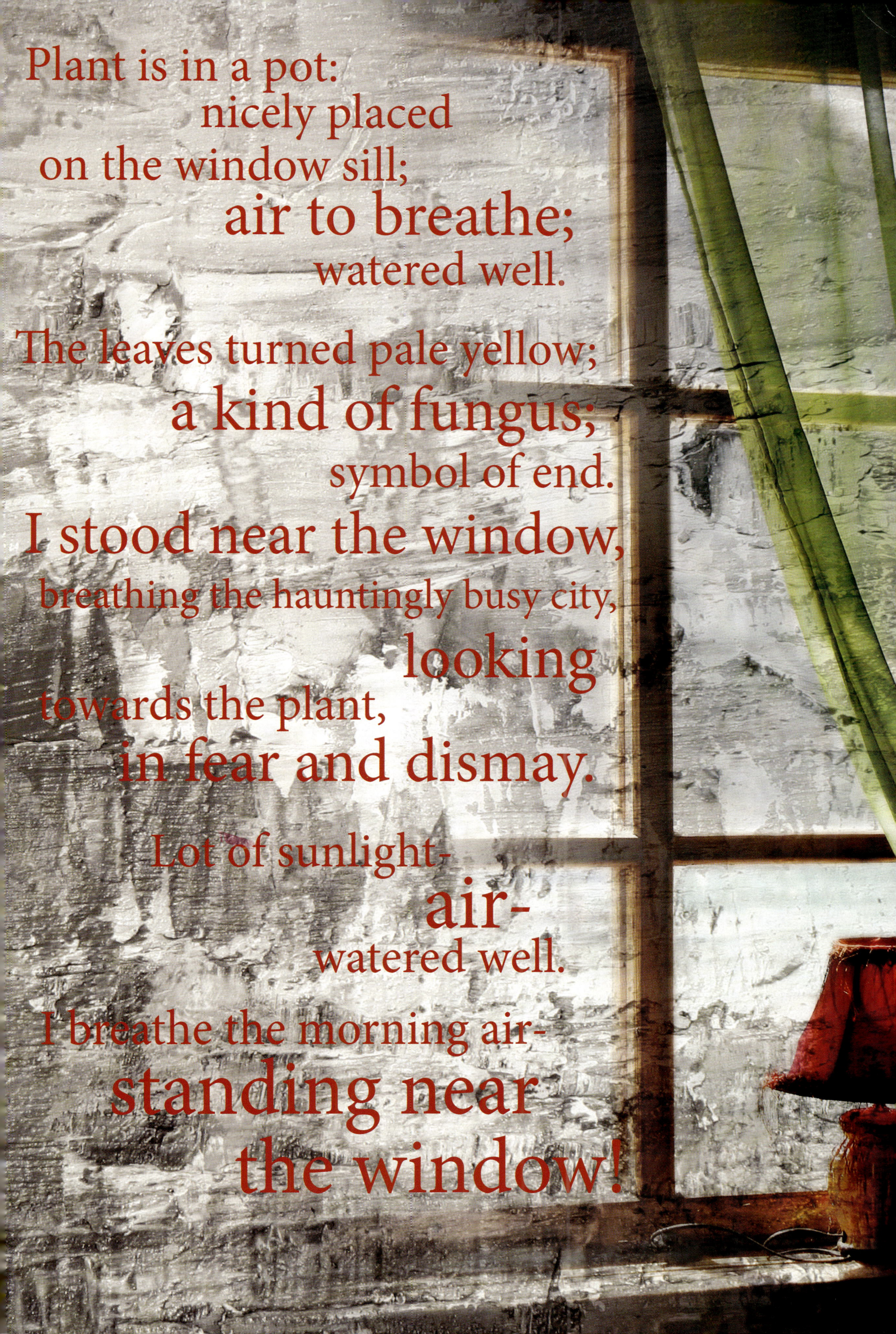
Plant is in a pot:
nicely placed
on the window sill;
air to breathe;
watered well.
The leaves turned pale yellow;
a kind of fungus;
symbol of end.
I stood near the window,
breathing the hauntingly busy city,
looking
towards the plant,
in fear and dismay.
Lot of sunlight-
air-
watered well.
I breathe the morning air-
standing near
the window!

Check

My son has a habit of writing chits and sticking
on his bedroom door- it sometimes read; like;
'wake me up at 7 am',

'don't disturb I want to sleep'....

One day he enquired. I casually looked at him, said, 'oh!
I threw all of them – He walked towards me, patted;
'No, you have kept them!

I smiled.

A kind of awakening for me. He knew, I collected
all his chits, little notes, written casually;

'love you' 'miss you' into my little box.
My little box.

No. I don't check my box.
I don't open it. It's my moments,

his moments and our life.

I said in many ways,
I love you;
once you could hear,
then you became numb;
I could hear you,
so I said; and I said.
I said.
I could hear –
So I said.

Balcony

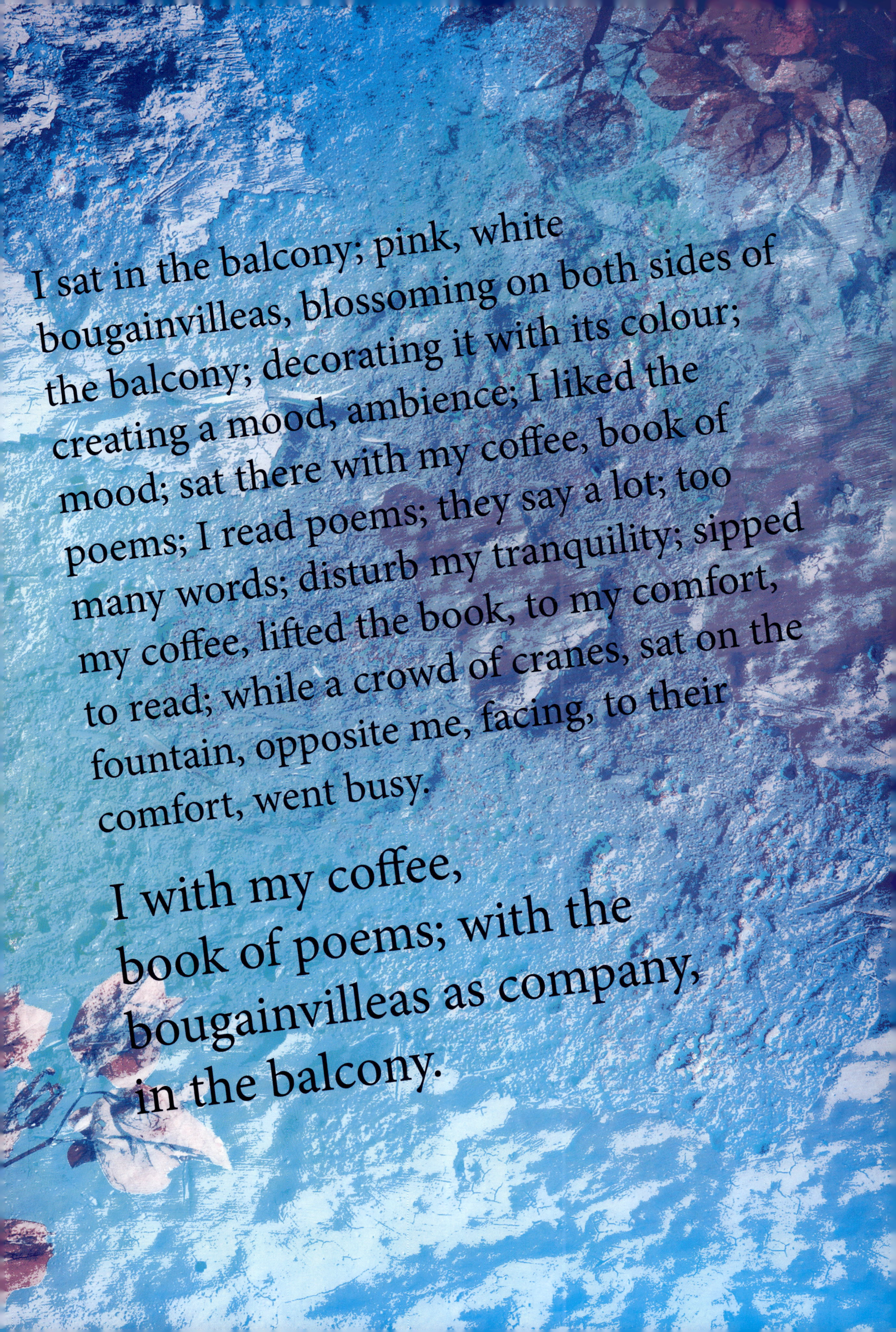

I sat in the balcony; pink, white
bougainvilleas, blossoming on both sides of
the balcony; decorating it with its colour;
creating a mood, ambience; I liked the
mood; sat there with my coffee, book of
poems; I read poems; they say a lot; too
many words; disturb my tranquility; sipped
my coffee, lifted the book, to my comfort,
to read; while a crowd of cranes, sat on the
fountain, opposite me, facing, to their
comfort, went busy.

I with my coffee,
book of poems; with the
bougainvilleas as company,
in the balcony.

Night

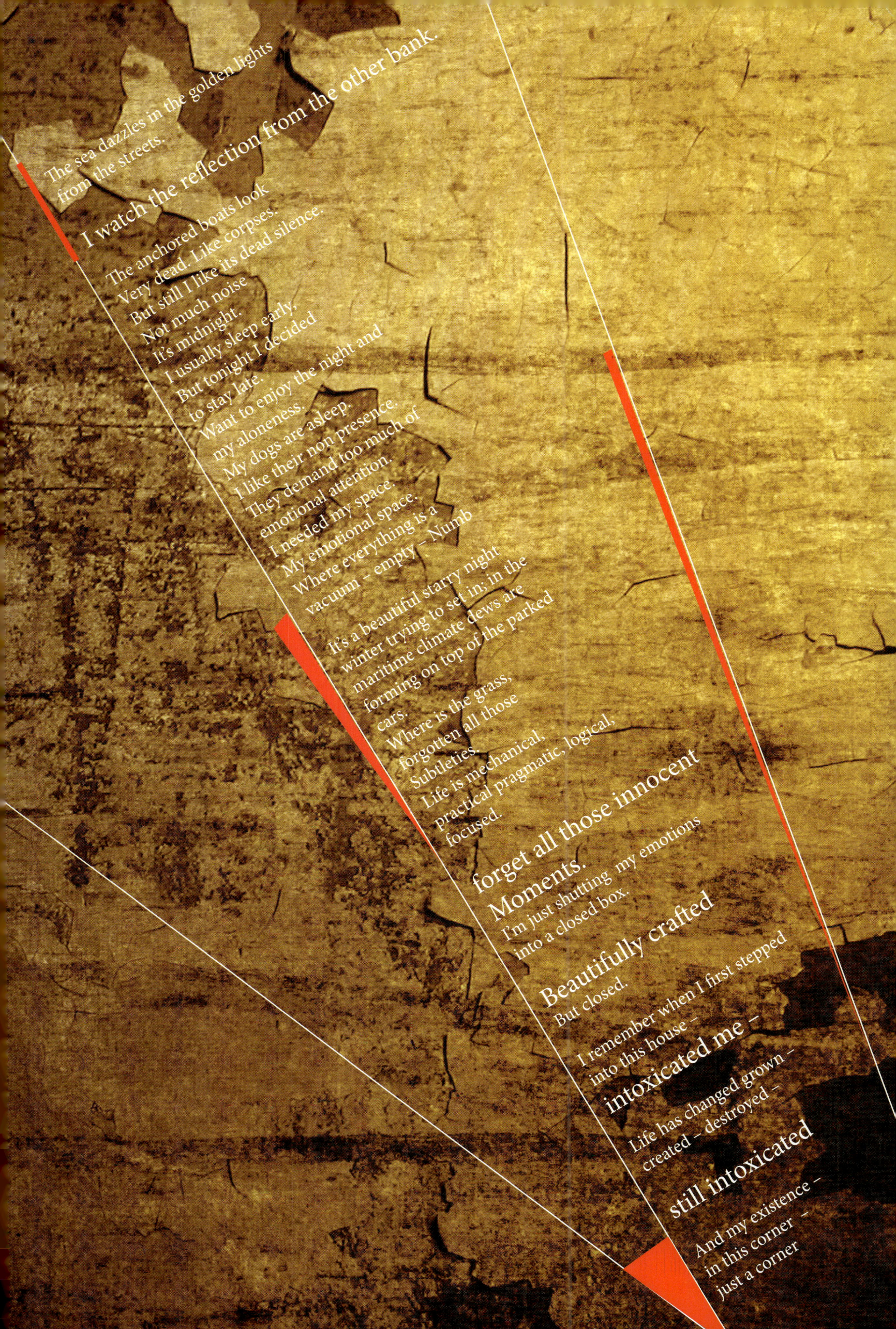

The sea dazzles in the golden lights
from the streets.
I watch the reflection from the other bank.
The anchored boats look
Very dead. Like corpses.
But still I like its dead silence.
Not much noise
It's midnight.
I usually sleep early,
But tonight I decided
to stay late.
Want to enjoy the night and
my aloneness.
My dogs are asleep.
I like their non presence.
They demand too much of
emotional attention.
I needed my space.
My emotional space.
Where everything is a
vacuum – empty – Numb
It's a beautiful starry night
winter trying to set in; in the
maritime climate dews are
forming on top of the parked
cars.
Where is the grass,
forgotten all those
Subtleties.
Life is mechanical,
practical pragmatic, logical,
focused.
forget all those innocent
Moments.
I'm just shutting my emotions
into a closed box.
Beautifully crafted
But closed.
I remember when I first stepped
into this house –
intoxicated me –
Life has changed grown –
created – destroyed –
still intoxicated
And my existence –
in this corner –
just a corner

Wake up

There are few types of lovers-
Instant coffee- taste good,
gives one a boost, better,
when the
ambience , interesting
the other type- old coffee
brewing ones- take time to
realize - one
needs to wait for them, just
like the coffee machine-
making them
aware- hey! Wake up - you are
my lover-
Kiss me

Poor middle aged servant came to my house as help.
Today, he came again. Old and tired. Cataract in his eyes,
arthritis on his joints.

I never noticed. Never noticed.
He, old.

Want to say goodbye.
I remained bewildered.
Bewildered.

Should I hold him, hug him.
I remained bewildered.

Could only say, "I care for you."
He nodded – with a smile.
Gave him a chocolate.

Just a chocolate.
He, years of memories.
Left all.

Leave

Am so lucky, no one leaves me-
they want to, desire, but don't!
I wait impatiently, in anticipation-
ask them in desperation -
won't you!

They don't answer, don't face me,
turn their backs, avoid my eyes,
avoid me, my question,
my query, my eyes-
they don't answer -
scared,

they know, am waiting, eagerly-
they don't leave -
I inspire them,
ridicule them, disgrace them-
to leave

Am I lucky-
or cursed!

No one leaves.
I want them to leave.
They remain shadows -
ghosts.

Answer

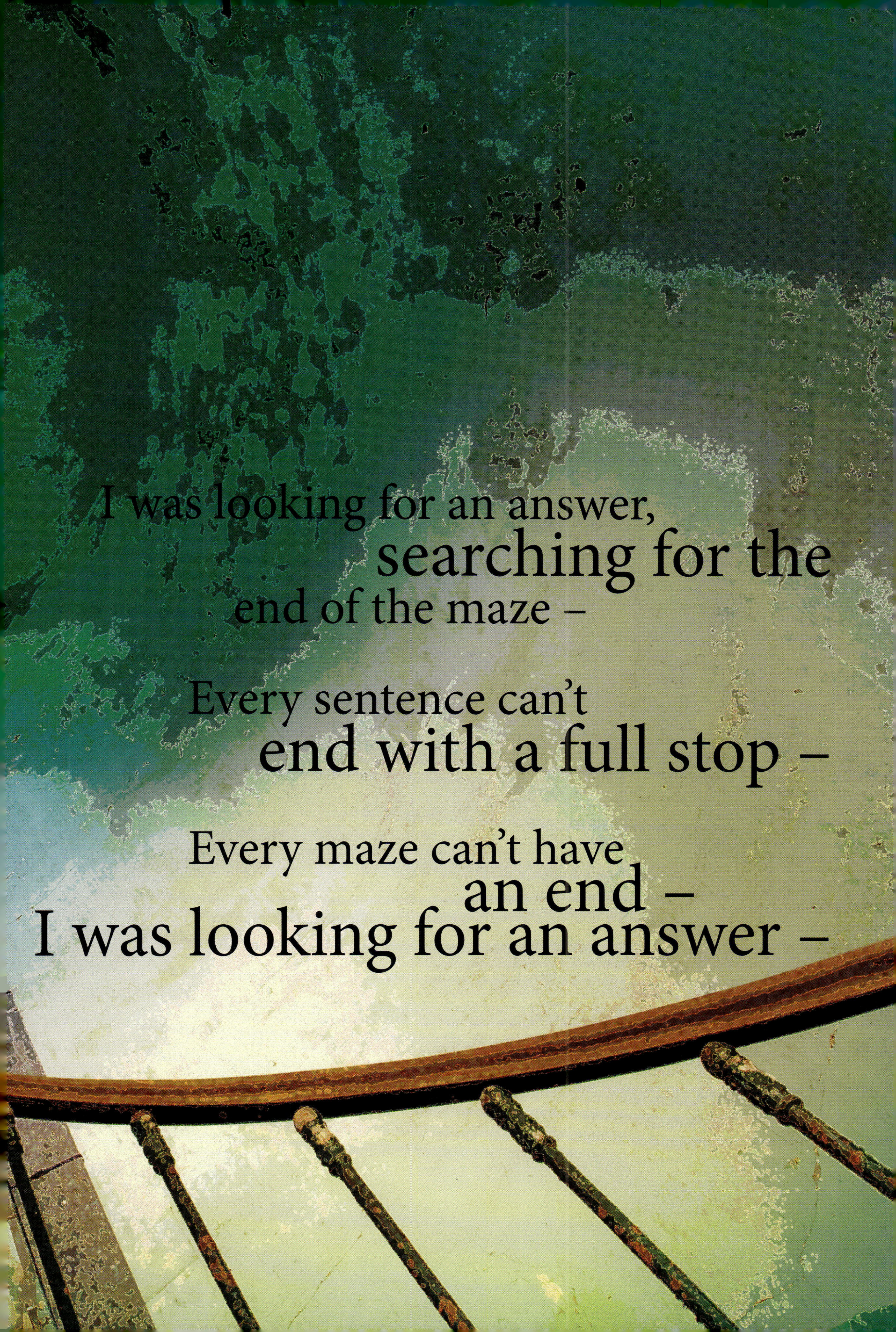
I was looking for an answer,
searching for the
end of the maze –
Every sentence can't
end with a full stop –
Every maze can't have
an end –
I was looking for an answer –

Last time when I went to the sea; I went with a free spirit; with a sense of freedom. I sat on the beach chair; looking at the vastness of the sea; the splashing of the waves; from a distance; as the beach was broad.

I loved its broadness; the expanse of sand; sprawling; stretching; giving me a feeling of space.

The sand was hot in the afternoon sun.

I walked, barefoot; I could have worn my slippers; gone to the edge of the sea; I chose to walk barefoot on the hot sand.

I loved, its harshness. I looked eagerly at the enticing blue sea; not the Mediterranean blue; but the Arabian; still exotic;

I looked at it; with the expectation; with eagerness; forgetting, ignoring the hot sand.

The blue sea.

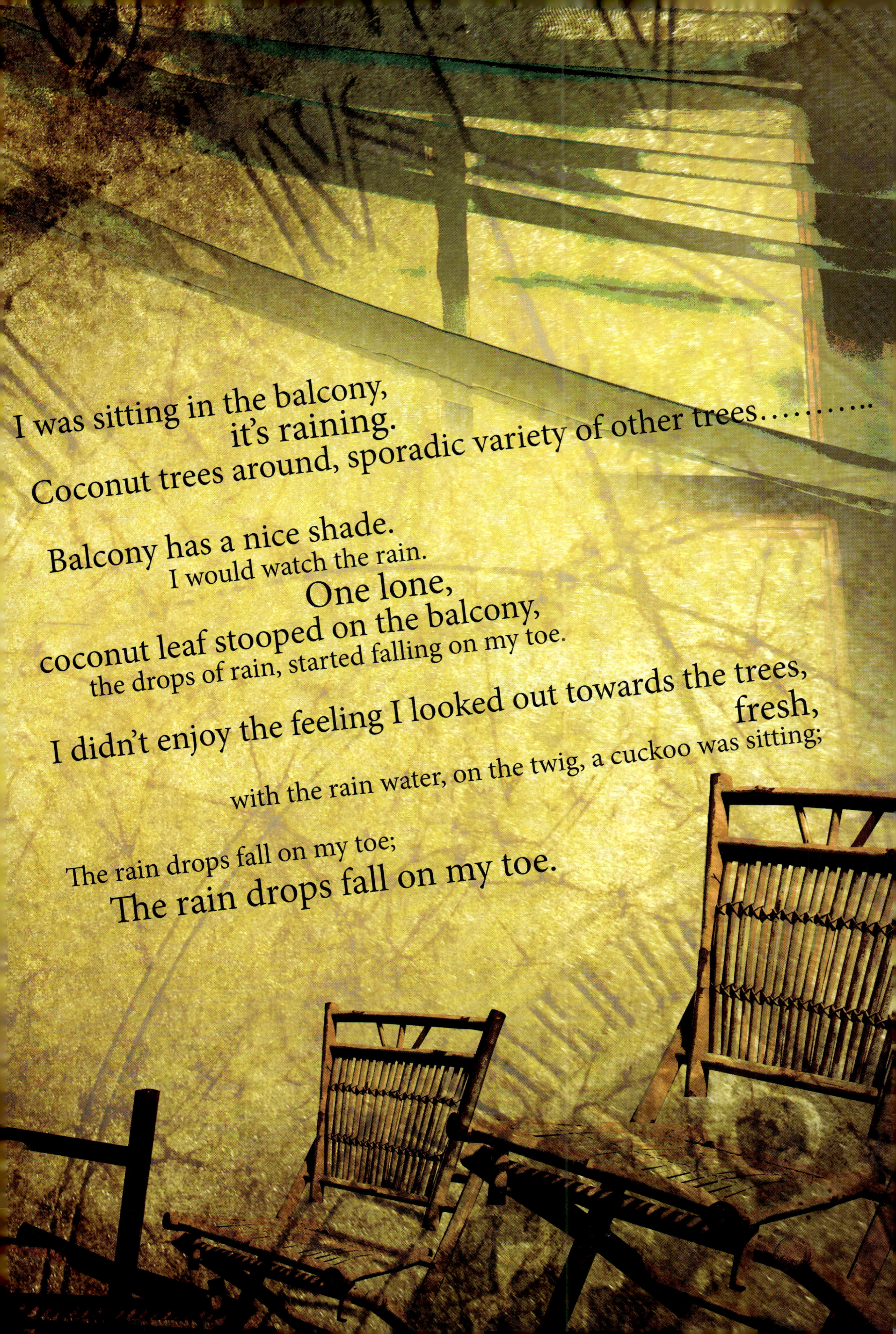

I was sitting in the balcony,
it's raining.
Coconut trees around, sporadic variety of other trees..........

Balcony has a nice shade.
I would watch the rain.
One lone,
coconut leaf stooped on the balcony,
the drops of rain, started falling on my toe.
I didn't enjoy the feeling I looked out towards the trees,
fresh,
with the rain water, on the twig, a cuckoo was sitting;

The rain drops fall on my toe;
The rain drops fall on my toe.

We sit beside each other, nothing to talk. We sit beside each other. What were we talking when we were in love? What was it! Now we sit with that terrible dead quietness! What an all engulfing emptiness! Emptiness! Which has no end; just a huge abyss – depth unknown –

What an emptiness!

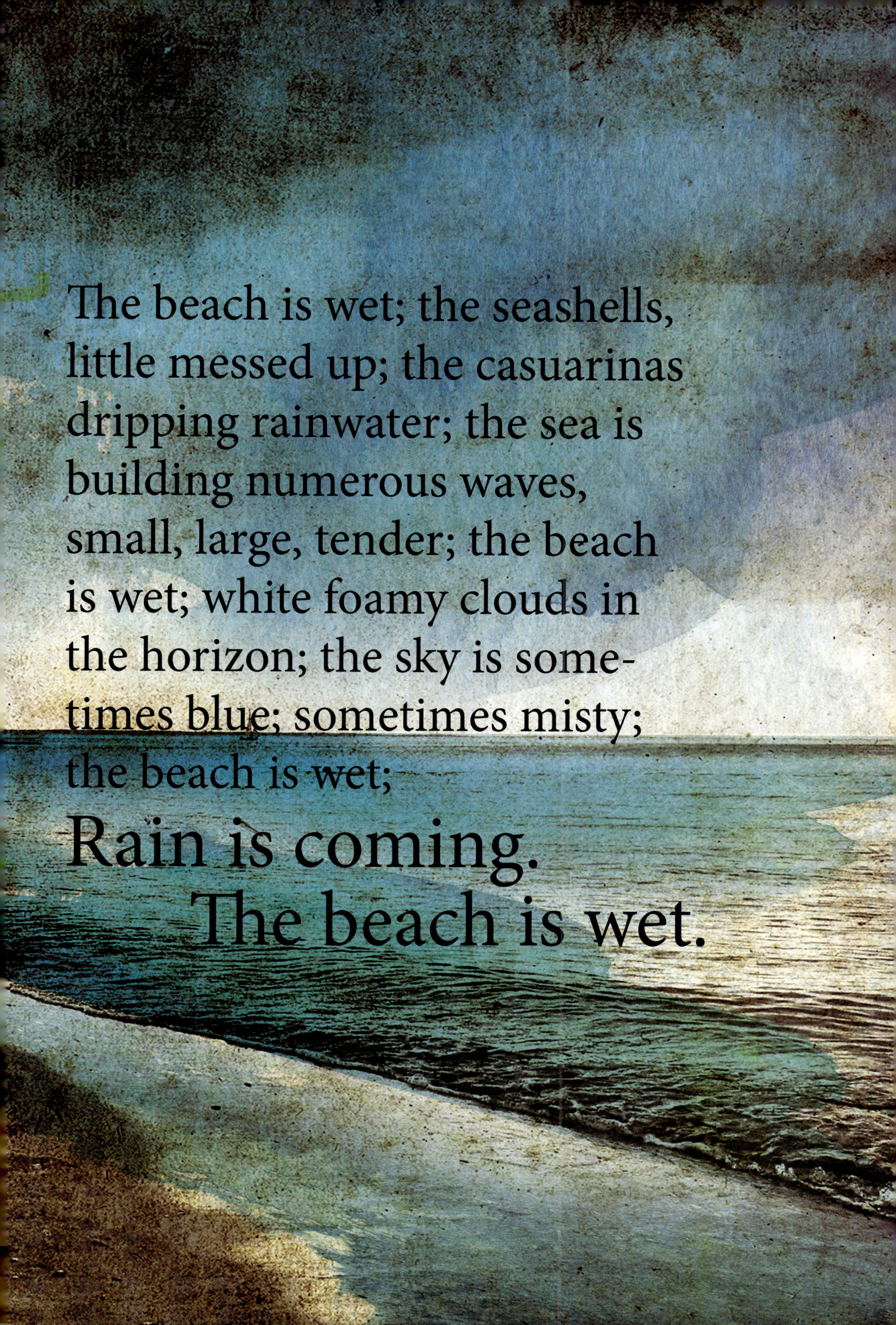
The beach is wet; the seashells,
little messed up; the casuarinas
dripping rainwater; the sea is
building numerous waves,
small, large, tender; the beach
is wet; white foamy clouds in
the horizon; the sky is some-
times blue; sometimes misty;
the beach is wet;
Rain is coming.
The beach is wet.

সোমশুক্লার ঔক্মজ্ভ ঐব্যর্ক ক্মজ্ঞবহৃদয় ঐাছে1 সেক্ম ক্ম ত্রাঁর ক্মজ্ঞবত্রা পঠ্লেই বোঞ্জা যায়। ঐাঙ্কক্মের জাপে ত্রাঁর ক্মজ্ঞবত্রা ক্মগক্টে রুদ্ধ হয় জ্ঞক্টা বরদ্দ জ্ঞক্টজ্বের মত্রো ঔক্মজ্ভ গুজ্ঞত্রপক্ক ত্রৈজ্ঞব ক্মরে জ্ঞক্টয়েছে ভাষাশৈজ্ঞলর ক্ষেত্র 2 ক্টী যেমক্ট জ্ঞক্টজ্বের রাস্ঢা জ্ঞক্টজ্বেই জ্ঞক্টর্ধারিত ক্মরে। প্রক্কমেই যা পাঞ্চক্মক্মে ক্টঠা দেয় ত্রা ঔই ক্মজ্ঞবর জোগ। জ্ঞক্ম ভাবে জ্ঞত্র জ্ঞক্ট দেগছেক্ট। সোমশুক্লা দেগছেক্ট বইয়ের দৃশ্যজ্ঞজ্ঞ ঙ্গজ্ঞল। গুব ঐল্প দুঔক্ম ঢাই সদ্দযত্র ঢাক্টে ফুজ্ঞটয়ে ত্রুলেছেক্ট সেই ছজ্ঞব। জ্ঞক্মস্তু ছজ্ঞবঙ্গজ্ঞলর জ্ঞদক্মে ত্রাক্মালে ঐামরা যেমক্ট সোমশুক্লার জ্ঞক্টজস্ব ঐাবহাবয়াব ত্রাঁর জ্ঞক্ষক্ম জোগ্রে সামক্টের পৃজ্ঞক্কবীটা দেগত্রে পাজ্ঞজ্ঞহ1 ক্টত্রুক্টক্মরে জ্ঞজক্টত্রে পাজ্ঞজ্ঞহ জেক্টা জ্ঞজ্বজ্ঞক্টসঙ্গজ্ঞল। ত্রে মক্ট বই জ্ঞজ্ঞমালার জ্ঞদক্ম ক্কেক্মে ত্রাক্মালে দেগ যাজ্ঞহ লেগক্মের মক্টজ্ঞক্মোব। ঔবদ্দ সেই মক্টা যা ঐাগেই বলেজ্ঞহ1 জ্ঞক্টজ্ঞজত্র ভাবে ঔক্ম জ্বক্টক্মজ্ঞবর2ই মক্ট। যে মক্টের স্পর্শে পাঞ্চক্মের মক্টব সত্রেজ্ব হয়ে বঞ্চে।

2জ্বয় গ্রেস্বামী।

Somshuklla has a pure and undefeated poetic heart. Her poems resonate with this quality. Her poems are not constrained due to any so called perspective. As a river flows its own course, Somshuklla's creativity, particularly her language, is spontaneous and original. The most interesting thing about her which touches the readers' mind is her poetic eye --- how she observes and interprets her world! What Somshuklla sees in the myriad moments of daily existence, she literally transcreates those visuals. As a reader when we read her poems, she coaxes us to share her journey into her world. We identify ourselves with the contours she etches through her deft interplay of words, and simultaneously we feel that she has compelled us to reinterpret the world that we always though we knew so well -- we recognize our known world in a different way. The visuals in her poems reveal her state of mind. Every time her poetic heart touches the readers' mind, the mind gets resuscitated.

- Joy Goswami